SHOCK ZONE™

DEADLY AND DANGEROUS

DEADLY Venomous ANIMALS

MATT DOEDEN

Lerner Publications Company • Minneapolis

Lerner Publications Company
A division of Lerner Publishing Group, Inc.
241 First Avenue North
Minneapolis, MN 55401 U.S.A.

Website address: www.lernerbooks.com

Library of Congress Cataloging-in-Publication Data

Doeden, Matt.
    Deadly venomous animals / by Matt Doeden.
        p.   cm. — (Shockzone™—deadly and dangerous)
    Includes index.
    ISBN 978–1–4677–0599–8 (lib. bdg. : alk. paper)
    1. Poisonous animals—Juvenile literature. I. Title.
QL100.D635 2013
591.6'5—dc23   2012018235

Manufactured in the United States of America
1 – PC – 12/31/12

TABLE OF CONTENTS

Imagine walking through a jungle, a swamp, or a desert. **Ouch!** Suddenly a sharp pain shoots through your leg. Something just bit you . . . or maybe stung you. Was it a snake? A spider? A scorpion? Whatever it was, your leg *hurts*! The skin turns red and starts to swell.

If you're lucky, all you'll get is a sore ankle. But what if the pain grows worse? Maybe it was no ordinary pest that attacked you. Maybe it was one of nature's most venomous animals. Deadly venom could be pumping through your veins. It could be making its way to your heart or your lungs. You might have days, hours, or only minutes to live. Death might be quick and painful— or slow and agonizing.

King cobras are the largest venomous snakes in the world.

4

What happens when the venom of a black widow rushes through you?

What kinds of animals can do this to you? Where do you find them? And most important, what do you do when one of them strikes? Turn the page to find out.

DEATH STALKER SCORPION

With a name like death stalker, it's no secret that this is a scorpion to avoid! This little monster proves that danger comes in small packages. The death stalker doesn't get much longer than 4 inches (10 centimeters). But don't let the small size fool you. These guys are *aggressive*. If they sense danger, they strike. And you don't want to be on the wrong end of that sting.

The death stalker creeps around the Middle East and North Africa. It's the world's most venomous scorpion. The death stalker's stinger pumps victims full of several powerful neurotoxins. These harsh chemicals attack the nervous system.

The nervous system controls a person's movements. It also sends signals from one part of the body to another. Neurotoxins scramble this system. The area that's stung swells up. Victims may get a bad fever, shake wildly, or fall into a coma. They may even become paralyzed and die.

paralyzed = unable to move

A type of medicine called antivenom can help victims bounce back from a death stalker sting. But victims need to get treated quickly. Even with the medicine, getting stung is an incredibly painful experience. And for children, the elderly, and people with heart problems, even the antivenom might not help.

antivenom = a medicine that protects victims from the effects of venom

Those who survive a death stalker sting are lucky. Still, victims never forget getting stung. Some animals have deadlier venom. But few can inflict as much pain as the death stalker.

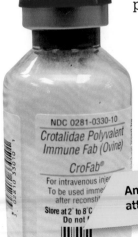

NDC 0281-0330-10
Crotalidae Polyvalent
Immune Fab (Ovine)
CroFab®
For intravenous injer
To be used imme
after reconsti
Store at 2˚ to 8˚C
Do not '

Antivenom is used to help victims attacked by venomous animals.

SYDNEY FUNNEL-WEB SPIDER

Australia's Sydney funnel-web spider is one critter you don't want to find in your bed. This spider is deadly and determined to protect its turf. That's a nasty combination.

Funnel-web spiders are burrowers. They build their funnel-shaped webs in dark, humid places—often under rocks or logs. But they are also wanderers—especially the males. Male funnel-web spiders move around at night searching for mates. In the daytime, they have to find a dark place to stay. Since this spider is less than 2 inches (5 cm) long, that place could be inside your shoe. If this critter does hide out in your kicks, get ready for an unpleasant time. The bite of a funnel-web spider can kill you if left untreated. Even if you do get treatment, your recovery won't be a lot of fun.

If a funnel-web spider decides to bite you, it goes all out. These spiders won't bite once and run. They'll keep biting and biting. Each bite injects a neurotoxin called robustoxin. This toxin is deadly only to primates. It doesn't affect other mammals. The spider's venom is made special to kill you! And the venom works fast. Years ago, a child reportedly died within fifteen minutes of a bite.

primates = mammals with feet and hands that can grab things

Sounds grim, but there's good news. In 1981 scientists developed an antivenom to defend against funnel-web spider venom. Since then, nobody has died from a funnel-web bite. More good news: female funnel-web spiders don't produce deadly venom. They're not quite so scary…if you know a way to tell the difference. Flipping a funnel-web over for a closer look is *not* recommended!

A scientist takes venom from a Sydney funnel-web spider to make antivenom.

King Cobra

The king cobra of Asia is one monster of a snake. It can grow up to 18 feet (5.5 meters) long. That makes it the longest venomous snake in the world! When threatened, king cobras use their long, powerful bodies to lift their heads. They puff out their famous hoods. Then they hiss. Imagine staring a giant hissing king cobra in the eye. Not fun.

But don't worry. King cobra usually avoid people. They strike only if provoked. (Life lesson: don't provoke a cobra!) They prefer to save their venom for their prey: other snakes. This diet is the

The king cobra's venom is a mix of neurotoxins and cardiotoxins. This venom is not that harmful compared to the venom of some other snakes. But the king cobra can inject *a lot* of it. The hurting starts when the snake sinks its 0.5-inch (1.25 cm) fangs into its victim. This is no quick strike. The king cobra often holds on, pumping more and more venom into its unlucky victim.

Healthy adults can easily survive a small king cobra bite. They may just suffer from severe pain and dizziness. But a bigger bite that isn't treated with antivenom can be deadly. When a cobra really unloads, it can pump 0.2 ounces (6 milliliters) of venom into its victim. That may not sound like a lot. But it's enough to kill twenty people or even an elephant!

The fangs of a king cobra help it cling to victims for a long bite.

STONEFISH

This ugly mug belongs to the most venomous fish in the world—the stonefish. The fish isn't pretty, but it's not the face that should worry you. A stonefish has thirteen sharp spikes on its back. Each spike is loaded with deadly venom.

Staying venom free should be simple. Just don't touch the spikes—right? If only it were that easy. Stonefish are burrowers. They nestle themselves down into mud, sand, or gaps between rocks. They also sport camouflage. If you're walking along the coast of

If you've been stung, you're in for one of the most painful experiences of your life. The sting starts with awful aching and swelling. Some victims suffer paralysis or go into shock. The venom is so toxic that all the tissue near the sting dies. Once a victim has been stung, the clock is ticking. Without treatment, he or she can be dead within an hour or two.

Even if a victim does get treatment, the horror isn't over. Tissue death can cause long-term problems. Some victims have scarring or permanent nerve damage. Other victims have reported such agony that they asked to have their limbs cut off. They'd rather lose a leg than deal with the pain!

protect your feet

Stonefish venom comes from spikes along the fish's back.

ARABIAN FAT-TAILED SCORPION

Take one look at the stinger on this little beast and you know it's gotta be trouble. That fat tail can hold a lot of venom. The Arabian fat-tailed scorpion's scientific name is *Androctonus crassicauda,* which means "man killer!" That alone ought to set off some warning bells.

This scorpion lives in desert regions of North Africa and the Middle East. It uses its venom to hunt insects. The venom also acts as a defense against enemies—including people. That's a problem, because this scorpion often makes its home in cities.

The fat-tailed scorpion is an ambush hunter. It's quick to

MAKING ANTIVENOM

So how is antivenom made? First, scientists take venom from an animal. Then they inject tiny bits of it into a mammal such as a goat or a horse. The animal's body learns to fight the venom. It creates cells called antibodies to protect itself. Scientists collect these antibodies and turn them into medicine.

An Arabian fat-tailed scorpion sting can kill a person within seven hours. A sting can kill a dog in as little as fifteen minutes! Stings are especially dangerous for children. The scorpion's venom attacks the nerves. Victims need antivenom to survive. Deaths from stings usually come from heart or lung failure.

Some people actually keep these scorpions as pets. But owning an Arabian fat-tail is very dangerous. Only experts in handling scorpions should do so. This is *not* the kind of pet you want a few feet from your bed!

Arabian fat-tailed scorpions live in the deserts of North Africa and the Middle East.

15

GREATER BLUE-RINGED OCTOPUS

Walking along the ocean, you notice a tiny octopus in a tide pool. It's no bigger than a golf ball. You lean in for a closer look. Suddenly the octopus's brown spots darken. Bright blue rings appear all over its body. What a beautiful sight.

Careful! This animal may be pretty, but it packs a mighty punch. Those bright blue rings are a warning. They're the octopus's way of telling you to back off. You do *not* want to be bitten by a blue-ringed octopus! Their saliva contains some of the deadliest venom on Earth.

A scientist holds a greater blue-ringed octopus in his hand. These venomous creatures are tiny!

The blue-ringed octopus hangs out near Pacific Ocean shores from Japan to Australia. It uses its strong neurotoxin to hunt small crabs and shellfish. The octopus busts through the shells of its prey with its strong beak. It can even snap through a diver's wetsuit.

Venom from the octopus's saliva blocks a victim's nerves from sending signals through the body. Victims can become paralyzed within minutes. They end up trapped in their own skin. They are awake and aware, but they can't move a muscle.

It's lights out if a person's lungs or the heart become paralyzed. Once those organs stop working, the only hope is a hospital. And what are the odds there's a hospital within a few minutes of the beach? The news only gets worse: there is no antivenom for a blue-ringed octopus bite. So do yourself a favor and give the cute little octopus plenty of room.

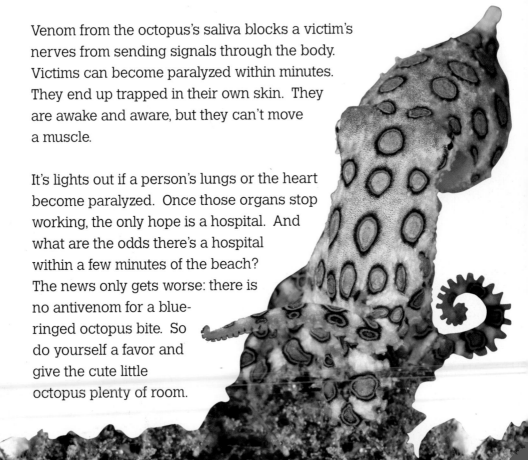

Inland Taipan

Many people call Australia's inland taipan the fierce snake. But the inland taipan isn't an aggressive animal. It does all it can to avoid people. The word *fierce* refers only to the snake's deadly venom. And that venom is fierce indeed.

Drop for drop, the inland taipan has the deadliest venom of any snake in the world. You wouldn't even need a full drop of it to die a quick, painful death. A single bite can inject enough venom to kill one hundred people. That's hardcore.

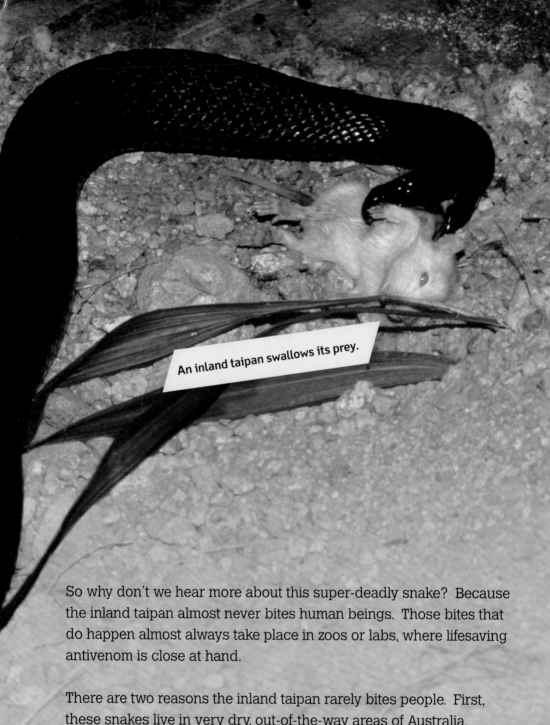

An inland taipan swallows its prey.

So why don't we hear more about this super-deadly snake? Because the inland taipan almost never bites human beings. Those bites that do happen almost always take place in zoos or labs, where lifesaving antivenom is close at hand.

There are two reasons the inland taipan rarely bites people. First, these snakes live in very dry, out-of-the-way areas of Australia. They rarely even meet humans. Second, the inland taipan is a timid creature. Even when they hunt, they avoid going head-to-head. They strike, retreat, and then wait for their prey to die. If threatened, they try to escape. They bite only as a last resort. So you've got to work pretty hard to get bitten by one. Still, it's best to avoid this bite!

Black Widow Spider

Few sights in the animal kingdom are scarier than the red hourglass pattern on the bottom of the black widow spider. These spiders live in warm areas all around the globe. Female black widows really earn their name. After they mate, some of them kill and eat the male!

Female black widows are a danger for humans too. Their venom is three times more powerful than the male's. Female black widows bite if threatened or if protecting a nest. A black widow injects its victim with nasty stuff called latrotoxin.

When a black widow bites a person, the venom quickly spreads through the person's body. It gets into the muscles and the nerves. It causes the victim's body to release a substance that stops muscles from relaxing. The victim goes through terrible muscle spasms. He or she can't relax the muscles, no matter what. Things get worse if the bite isn't treated. The victim can suffer kidney failure. Some fall into comas and die. Those who survive may have weeks or months of pain ahead of them.

spasm = an uncontrollable movement

STRONG AS STEEL

Black widows don't just boast deadly venom. They also spin some of the strongest silk in the world. A strand of black widow silk is as strong as a strand of steel wire of the same thickness. But the spider's silk is six times lighter. That means it's one of the strongest substances in nature.

This black widow uses its strong silk to trap a cricket.

GEOGRAPHIC CONE SNAIL

Spiders, snakes, scorpions—nobody would be too surprised to find them on a list of the world's most venomous animals. **But a snail?**

There are more than six hundred species of cone snails in the world. Most are harmless to humans. But a handful of species are deadly. The most dangerous is the geographic cone snail. These snails hunt fish, shellfish, and other critters on the bottoms of the Indian Ocean and the Pacific Ocean.

Cone snails have a needlelike body part called a radula. The snails can shoot it out of their mouths like a harpoon! A narrow tube connects a cone snail to its radula. The longest tube ever measured was 5 feet (1.5 m) long. And that was from a snail only 5 inches (13 cm) in length!

This geographic cone snail swallows a fish.

The cone snail has no interest in people. But many people find the snails' shells beautiful. They pick them up for a closer look and *bam*! Out comes the radula. The snail pumps its victim full of conotoxin, a fast-acting neurotoxin. The first symptoms of a sting are pain and swelling. The area may go numb. The victim may experience vision problems and paralysis. In the worst cases, the paralysis can spread to the lungs. Without a trip to the hospital, that's a death sentence.

HELPFUL VENOM?

The cone snail's venom has some nasty effects. Even so, the venom is also helpful in making medicine. Scientists have used it to create powerful painkillers. Cone snail venom may also be useful in creating medicines to treat nerve diseases such as Parkinson's disease.

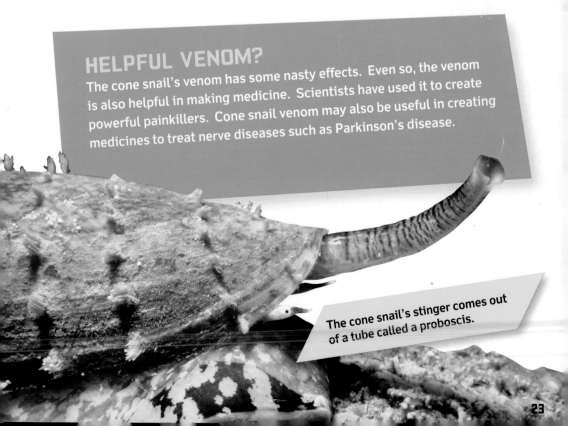

The cone snail's stinger comes out of a tube called a proboscis.

BRAZILIAN WANDERING SPIDER

If you thought the black widow sounded creepy, wait til' you meet the Brazilian wandering spider. Its **venom is five times deadlier** than the black widow's!

These spiders live in Central America and South America. But sometimes they hitch a ride north in shipments of bananas, pineapples, or other fruits. There's a reason they're called wandering spiders. It's because they wander around at night, looking for prey. During the daytime, they find dark, cool places to hide. Like inside a nice crate filled with bananas. So if you see a big, hairy spider crawling on your fruit, back off!

The Brazilian wandering spider delivers two kinds of bites. One is a dry bite. This bite is just a warning. The spider doesn't release any venom—it's saving that for prey. Dry bites hurt, but they're not dangerous. The trouble comes when the spider decides that you're worth spending some venom on. If wandering spiders feel seriously threatened, they pump victims full of as much venom as they can. And that's big-time bad news. Without antivenom, a wet bite can mean death. Even with it, you're looking at weeks of awful pain. In other words, hope for the dry bite!

Brazilian wandering spiders can hitch rides in shipments of pineapples!

Coral Snake

Want to meet a deadly snake without leaving North America? Look no further than the coral snake. It's a beauty of a reptile. But don't let the snake's good looks fool you. Those bright colors are nature's warning. The coral snake is one of the most dangerous creatures in North America.

Coral snakes live in warm parts of North America. They're common from California to Texas to Florida. Coral snakes hunt small animals such as mice and frogs. They don't have much interest in people. They'll try to flee before they bite. But if you push them too far, they will strike. And coral snakes tend to hold onto you once they sink in their teeth. You'll need to pry off a snake before it

The coral snake *(top)* is poisonous, but the kingsnake *(bottom)* is not.

Some less deadly snakes mimic the North American coral snake. The coral snake has bands of yellow between its black and red. Kingsnakes and milk snakes have the same colors as coral snakes but in reverse order. So remember this rhyme: red on yellow, kill a fellow; red on black, venom lack.

mimic = to take after or imitate

It's a simple way to spot a real coral snake. If the red and black bands don't touch, stay away!

This coral snake chows down on a rough earth snake.

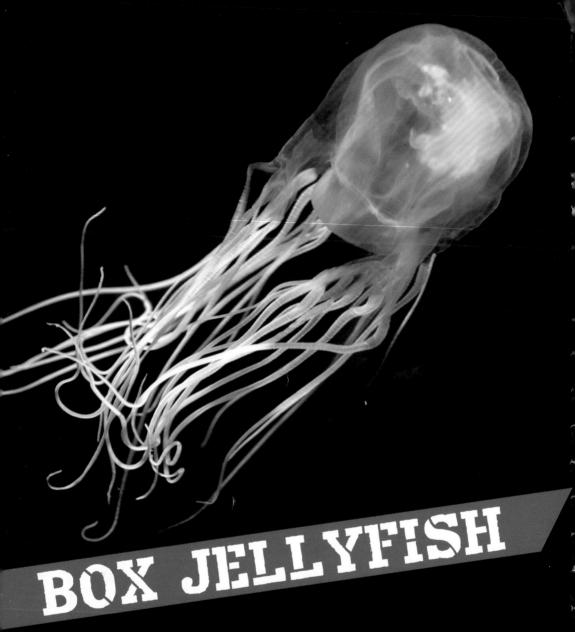

BOX JELLYFISH

The box jellyfish doesn't look too tough. But its sting packs a mighty punch. No joke—this creature's venom is deadlier than that of any other animal. The box jellyfish hangs out in the Pacific Ocean. Its venomous touch has earned it the nickname sea wasp.

Jellyfish bodies are light and delicate. That's why their venom is so deadly. The box jellyfish hunts fish. It needs to kill them very quickly. A thrashing fish could tear a jellyfish to pieces. So the box jellyfish has developed some hardcore venom for ultrafast kills.

The first danger to people who come into contact with the jellyfish comes from a substance called a dermonecrotic. It's a toxin that eats away at the skin like acid. Some stings are so painful that victims pass out and drown!

The hurting doesn't stop there. Box jellyfish venom also contains neurotoxins and cardiotoxins. These toxins attack the nerves and the heart. Victims can suffer heart attacks within minutes of a sting. Or their lungs can stop working.

The strength of a box jellyfish sting depends on a few things. One is the size of the jellyfish. The bigger the animal, the worse the sting. Another is the number of tentacles that touch the victim. More tentacles mean more suffering. Light stings may just leave a person with some scars. But a big sting is an almost guaranteed death sentence. So keep your distance. Just because it looks harmless doesn't mean that it is!

tentacles = long, narrow body parts that stretch out beyond the main body of a jellyfish

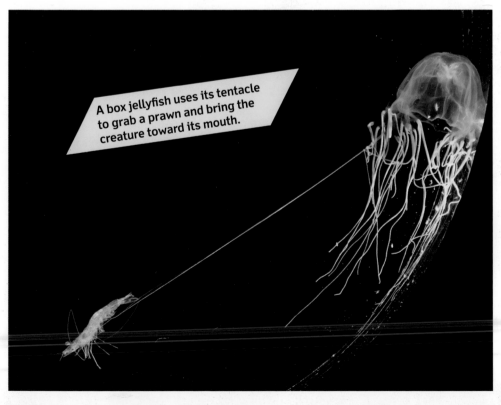

A box jellyfish uses its tentacle to grab a prawn and bring the creature toward its mouth.

FURTHER INFORMATION

Bodden, Valerie. *Scorpions.* Mankato, MN: Creative Education, 2011.
Dive into the wild world of scorpions in this book. Colorful photos and text reveal some of the coolest scorpions on Earth.

Harris, Tim, ed. *Venomous Snakes.* New York: Gareth Stevens, 2010.
Learn more about a wide range of venomous snakes. Discover what makes snake venom so dangerous and how to recognize venomous species.

Insect Bites and Stings: First Aid
http://www.mayoclinic.com/health/first-aid-insect-bites/FA00046
Do you know what to do if you're bitten or stung? Check out the Mayo Clinic's recommendations on how to treat a variety of bites and stings.

Johnson, Sylvia A. *Cobras.* Minneapolis: Lerner Publications, 2007.
Check out this book to read about cobras, their habits, and how they use venom to hunt and kill prey.

Lunis, Natalie. *Deadly Black Widows.* New York: Bearport, 2009.
People have always been fascinated by the beauty and danger of the black widow. Learn all about these amazing spiders, their habitats, hunting methods, and deadly venom.

10 Venomous Creatures in Your Backyard
http://www.howstuffworks.com/environmental/life/zoology/all-about-animals/10-venomous-creatures.htm
You don't have to go to exotic locations to find venomous animals. Learn about venomous animals that you might find in your own backyard.

White, Nancy. *Diamondback Rattlers: America's Most Venomous Snakes!*
New York: Bearport, 2009.
The diamondback rattlesnake didn't make our list of most venomous animals, but it's one of the deadliest animals in North America. Photos and text reveal what makes this snake a serious, slithery danger.

World's Most Venomous Animals—*Cosmos* Magazine
http://www.cosmosmagazine.com/features/online/5131/worlds-most-venomous-animals
Cosmos magazine offers its list of the world's most venomous animals. Read more about some of the deadliest creatures on Earth.

LERNER

SOURCE

Expand learning beyond the printed book. Download free, complementary educational resources for this book from our website, www.lerneresource.com.

PHOTO ACKNOWLEDGMENTS

The images in this book are used with the permission of: © Bruce Davidson/naturepl.com, p. 4; © GK Hart/Vikki Hart/Stone/Getty Images, p. 5; © Stephen Dalton/Photo Researchers, Inc., p. 6; © Ricardo Ramirez Buxeda/Orlando Sentinel/MCT via Getty Images, p. 7; © Ian Waldie/redbrickstock.com/Alamy, p. 8; © iStockphoto.com/pearleye, p. 9 (top); © Roland Seitre/naturepl.com, p. 9 (bottom); © Simon King/naturepl.com, p. 10; © Mattias Klum/National Geographic/Getty Images, p. 11 (both); © Hal Beral/Visual&Written SL/Alamy, p. 12; © Jurgen Freund/naturepl.com, pp. 13 (top), 17 (bottom); © David Doubilet/National Geographic/Getty Images, pp. 13 (bottom), 29; © Wigbert Roth/imagebroker/CORBIS, p. 14; © Naftali Hilger/arabianEye/Getty Images, p. 15 (background); © Hybrid Images/Cultura/Getty Images, p. 15 (inset top); © Barbara Strnadova/Photo Researchers, Inc., p. 15 (inset bottom); © Chris Newbert/Minden Pictures, p. 16; © Jeff Rotman/naturepl.com, pp. 17 (top), 23 (bottom); © Jason Edwards/National Geographic/Getty Images, p. 18; © Michael Dick/Animals Animals, p. 19; © John Giustina/CORBIS, p. 20; © Scott Camazine/Alamy, p. 21; © Reinhard Dirscherl/Visuals Unlimited, Inc., p. 22; © Alex Kerstitch/Visuals Unlimited, Inc., p. 23 (top); © Joao Paulo Burini/Flickr Open/Getty Images, p. 24; © Ze Paiva/LatinContent/Getty Images, p. 25 (top); © Amanda Vivan/Flickr/Getty Images, p. 25 (bottom); © Todd Pusser/Minden Pictures, p. 26; © Jeffrey Lepore/Photo Researchers, Inc., p. 27 (top); © Paul Freed/Animals Animals, p. 27 (bottom); © Melanie Stetson Freeman/The Christian Science Monitor/Getty Images, p. 28.

Front cover: © iStockphoto.com/Omar Ariff.

Main body text set in Calvert MT Std Regular 11/16.
Typeface provided by Monotype Typography.